Dear Asshole: Sarcastic Insult and Swear Word Coloring Book

Sassy Quotes Press

SassyQuotesPress.com

Sign up for freebies, prize giveaways, new releases and discounts at SassyQuotesPress.com

Laugh, Color and Relax!

Get ready to entertain your creative brain with **30 hilarious swear word coloring designs**.

These super salty quote designs are printed on single-sided pages, so you can use your favorite colored pencils, gel pens or markers to create cool, frameable artwork — for yourself, or a friend!

Pro tip: If you're using pens or markers and want to be extra sure that your colors don't bleed through, put another sheet of paper or card stock behind the page you're coloring. You'll find color test pages in the back of the book so you can try out your colors.

Happy coloring!

P.S. A favor please! Would you take a quick minute to *leave us a rating/review on Amazon*? It makes a HUGE difference and we would really appreciate it.

Thank you!

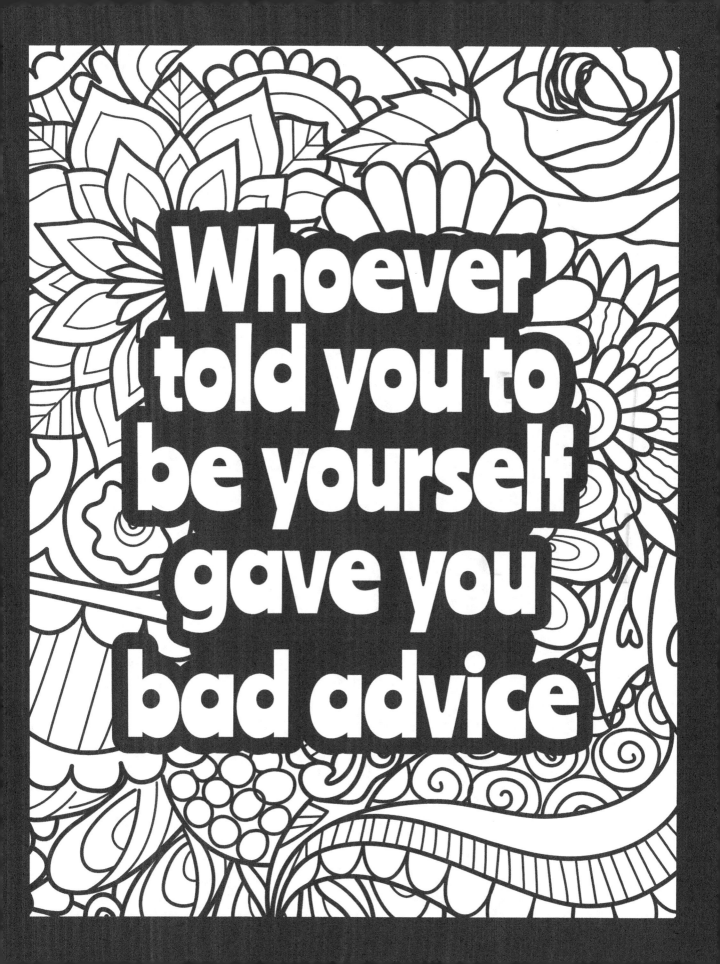

I'm not insulting you.

I'm describing you.

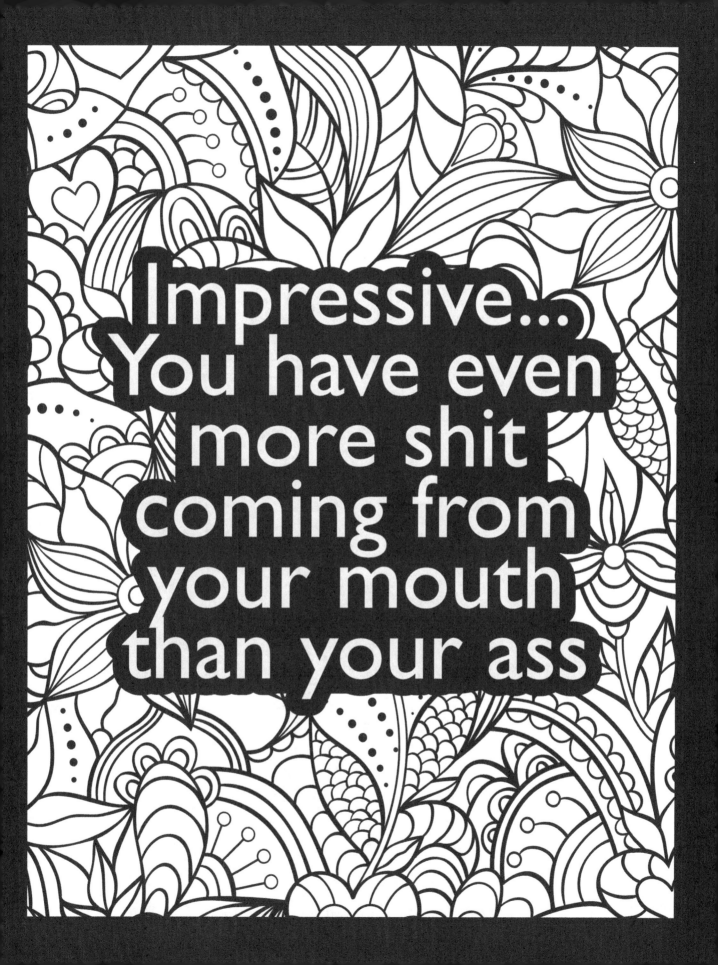

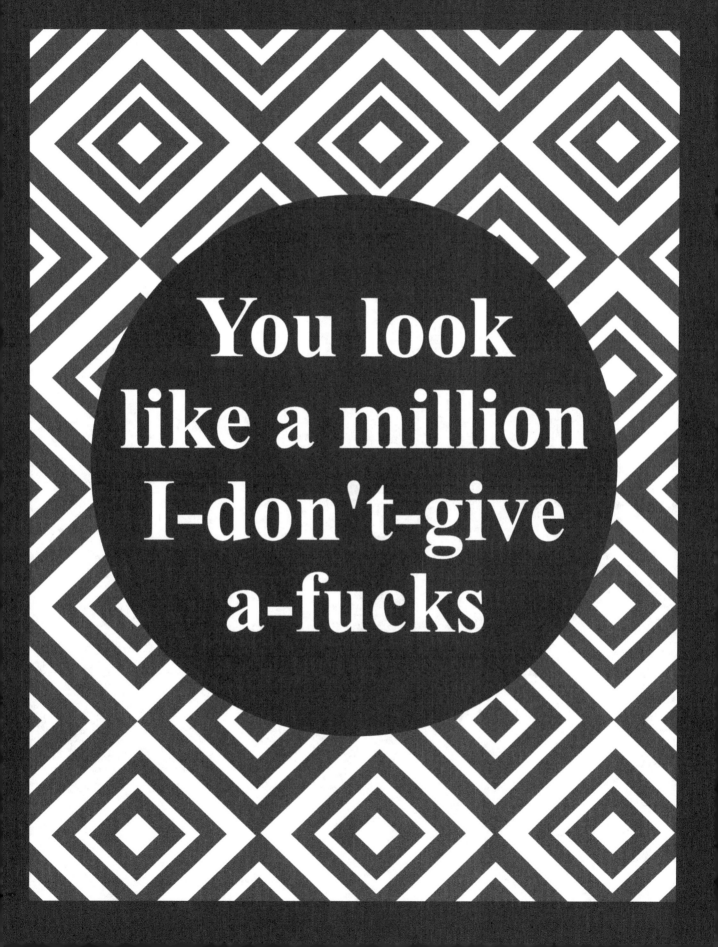

I can explain it to you

But I can't understand it for you

I don't have an
attitude problem

You have a
perception problem

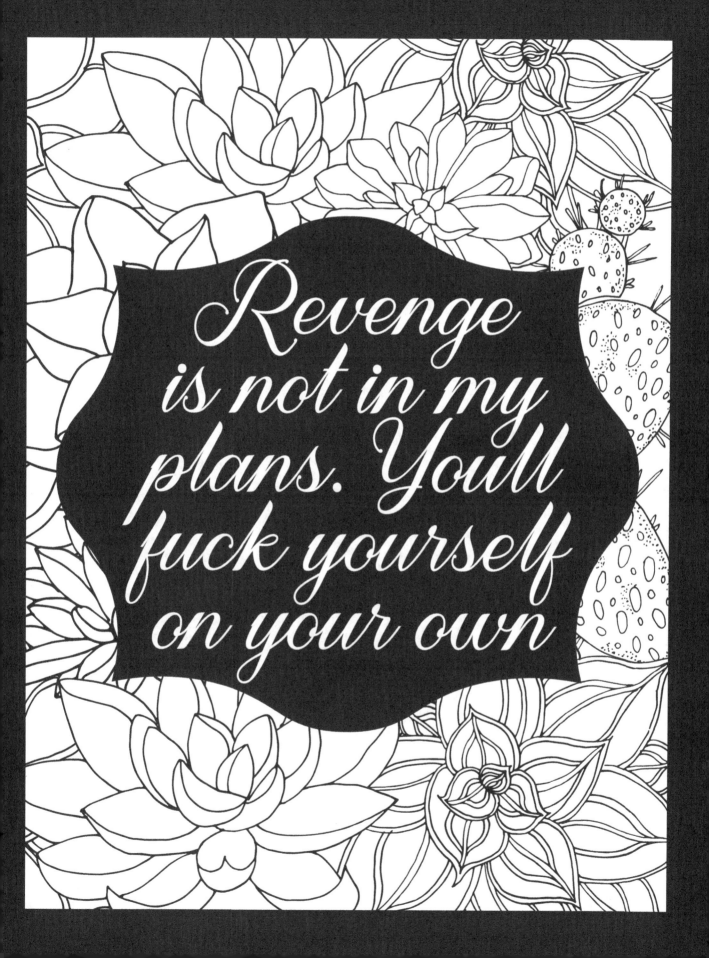

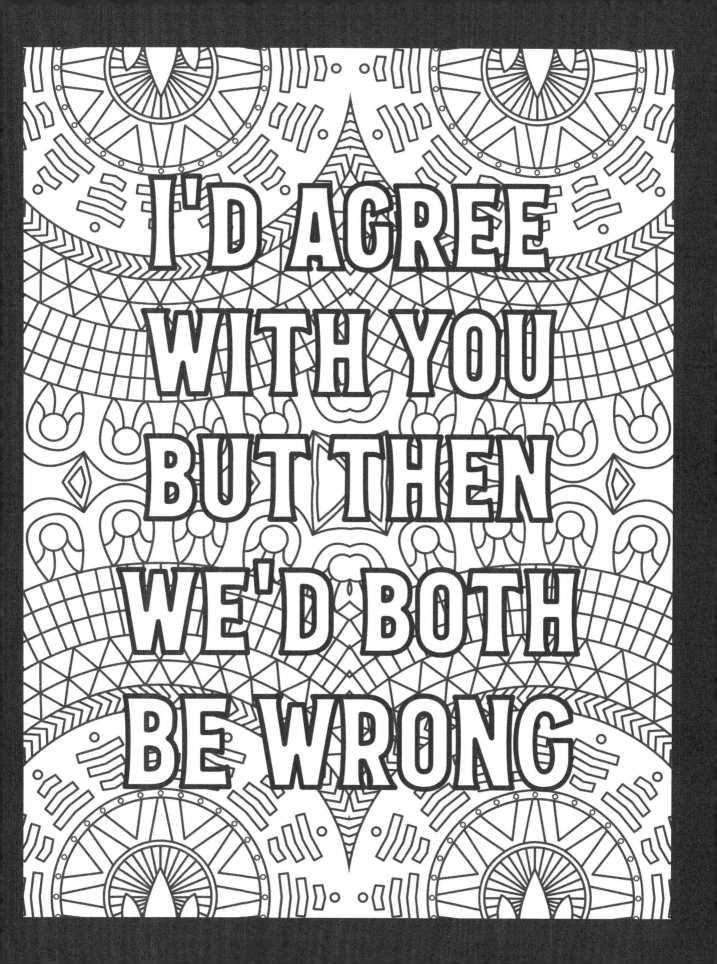

When I said, "How stupid can you be?" it wasn't a challenge

Keep rolling your eyes Mabye you'll find your brain back there

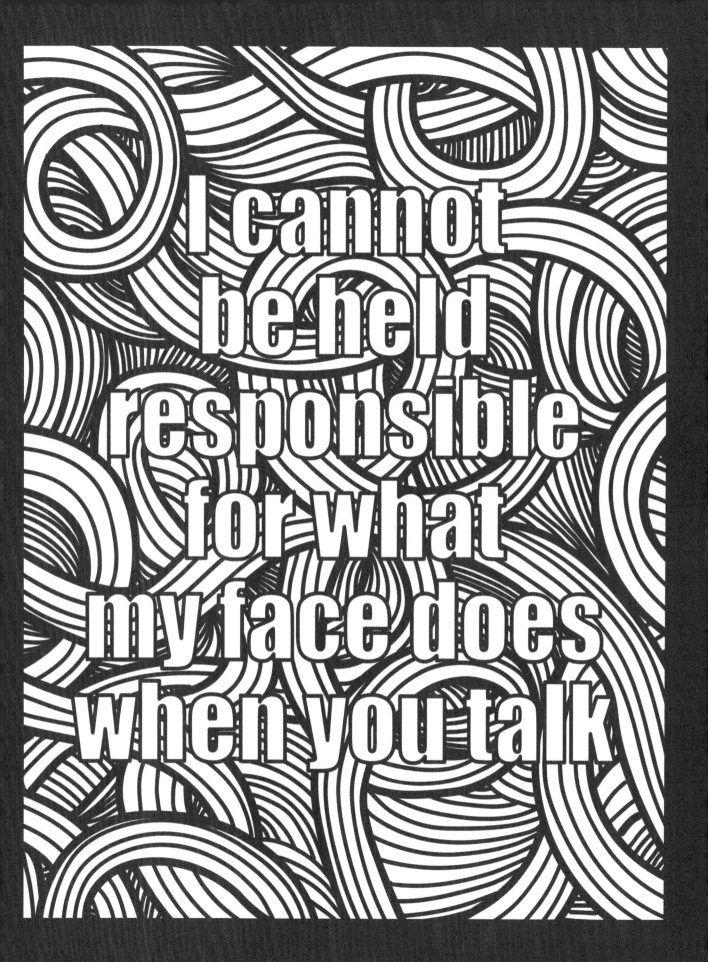

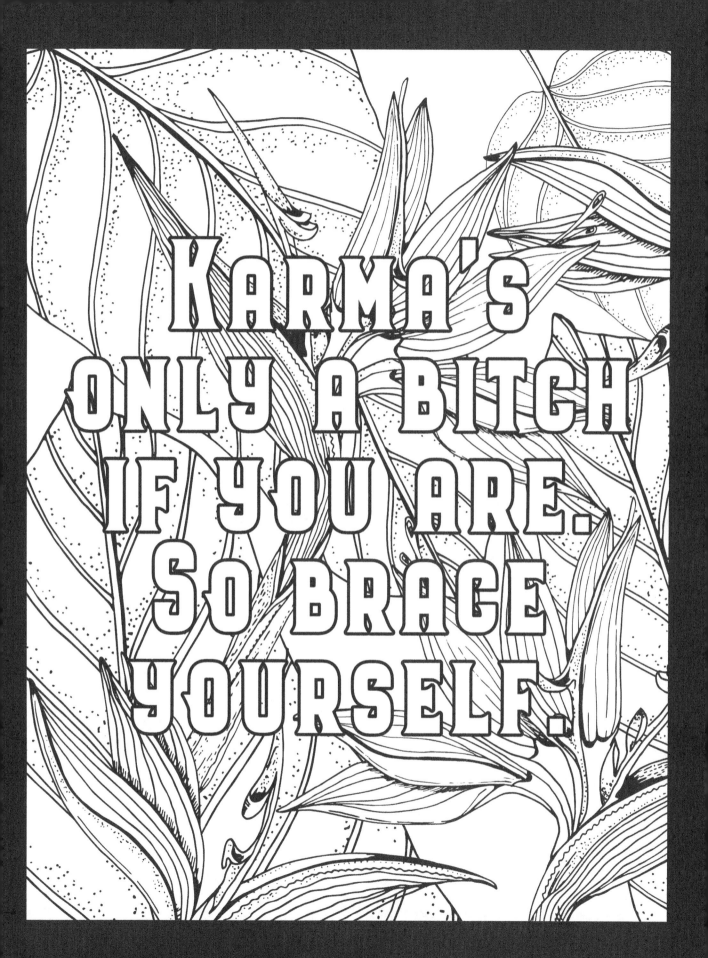

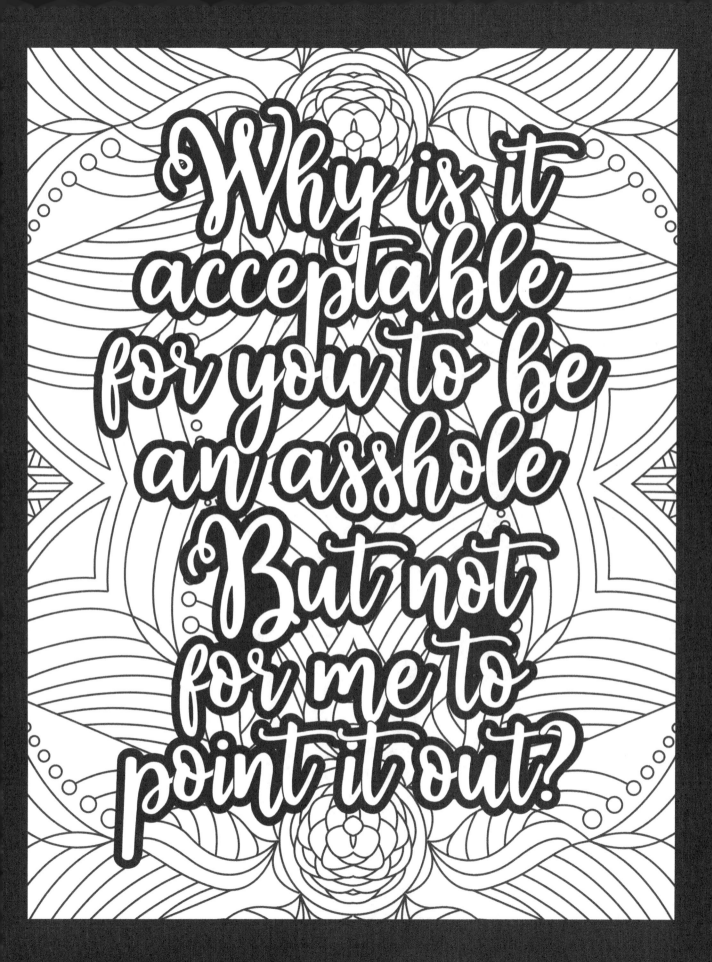

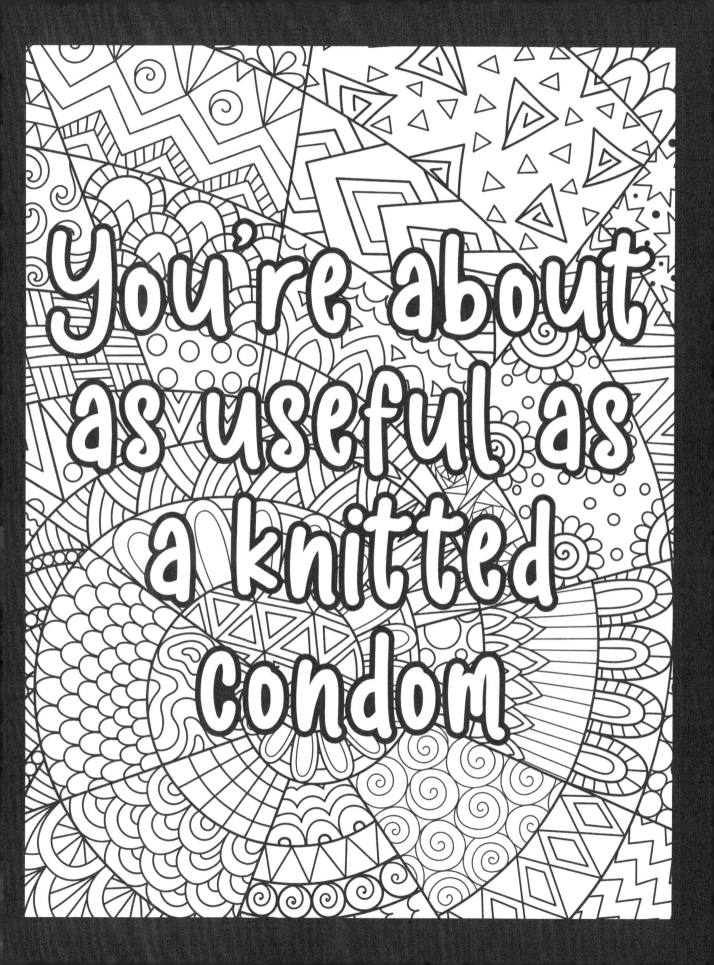

If you find me offensive, then I suggest you stop finding me.

I don't hate you. I'm just not excited about your existence.

I didn't mean to push your buttons. I was just looking for mute.

COLOR TEST PAGE

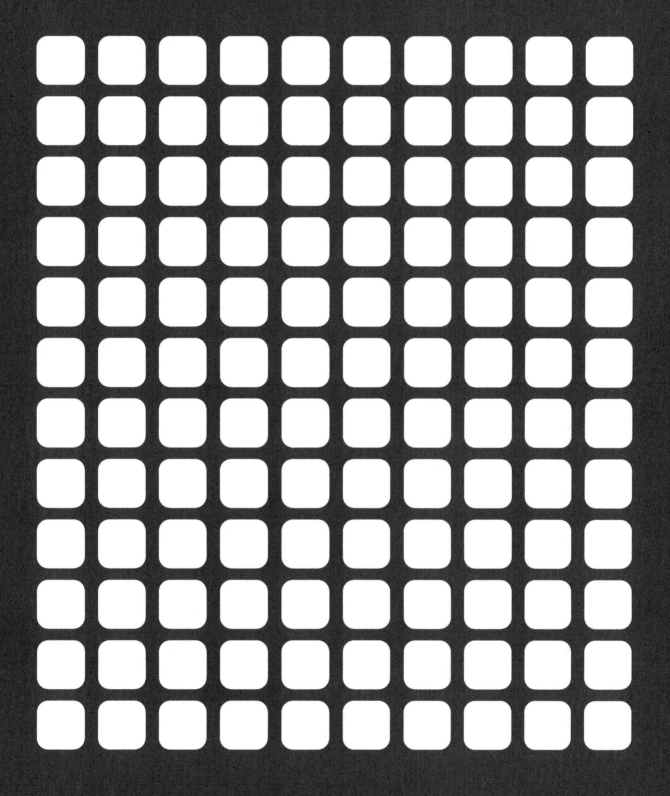

COLOR TEST PAGE

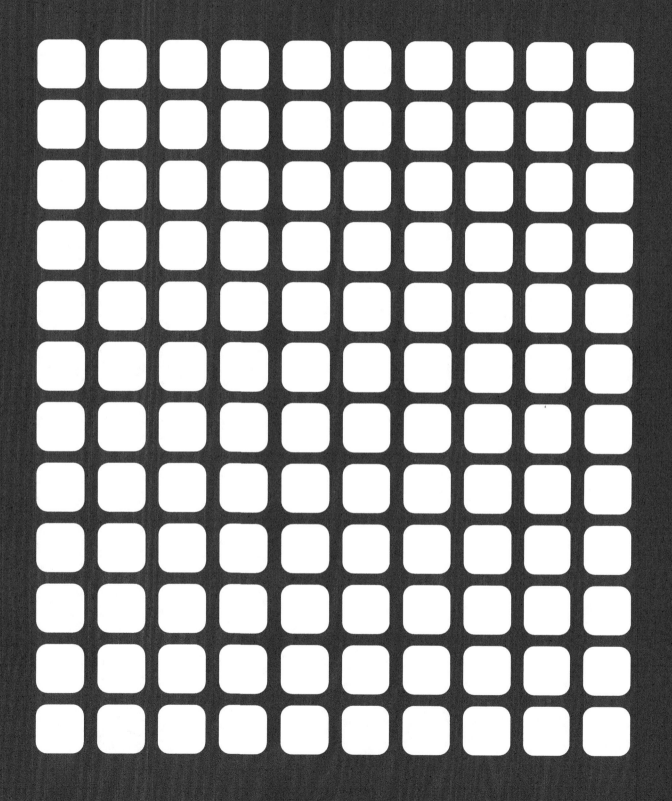

Hope you had fun coloring!

Want some coloring **freebies** to brighten your day?

Have comments or questions about our books?

Please visit us at
sassyquotespress.com

A favor please

Would you take a quick minute to leave us a rating/review on Amazon? It makes a *HUGE* difference and we would really appreciate it.

THANK YOU!

More Fun From Sassy Quotes Press

See these and more at
amazon.com/author/sassyquotespress

Cuss and Color: Swear Word Coloring Book

Cuss and Color: Swear Word Coloring Book (Midnight Edition)

Dear Asshole: Sarcastic Insults and Swear Words Coloring Book (Midnight Edition)

Dear Asshole at Work: Funny Swear Words Coloring Book (Midnight Edition)

Nice Job: Sarcastic Work Humor

Swearing? I Call it Strong Language

The World is My Toilet: Foul Mouthed Fowl Cussing Animals Coloring

Or scan this QR code with your device

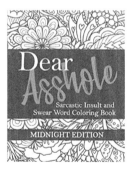

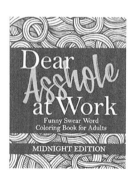

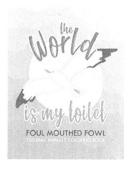

Made in the USA
Middletown, DE
31 August 2024

60094481R00040